SCIENCE FOR ME

by
Linda Diebert

illustrated by Barbara Smart-Smith

Cover by Janet Skiles

Copyright © Good Apple, 1991

ISBN No. 0-86653-597-7

Printing No. 98765432

Good Apple
1204 Buchanan St., Box 299
Carthage, IL 62321-0299

Simon & Schuster Supplementary Education Group

DEDICATIONS

To my friend and partner Andra, who always keeps me moving ahead and smiling, and to my children Alyson and Eric, because I love them. Thanks for your patience and love.

Linda

To my lovely Shannon, who was always there when I needed her. To Kelly for making me laugh and Patrick, whose bad jokes, burnt toast and sweet smile light up my life. Love and kisses.

Barbi Sue

GA1318

Table of Contents

GA1318

Introduction

Young children have a natural curiosity and desire to learn the "how," "why," and "what" of the world around them. Science, with all its mystery and excitement, can be a natural extension of this desire for learning. Children learn by doing and experiencing the world around them. *Science for Me* is written for young children so that they can explore science the best way they know how—HANDS ON!

This book is designed so that each set of activity cards is ready for classroom use. Cards can be removed from the book, laminated for extra durability, and then set up in sequential order for the science activity.

Teacher information with each set of cards will help you gather your materials and prepare the experiment. Children can work in groups or individually as they progress through each step of the activity. Card numbers, written directions, and picture directions help students at all reading levels complete the activity successfully. Science "recipes" can also be enlarged on a large chart to enhance vocabulary and reading skills. Math skills grow too as children count, measure, and compare.

A suggested parent information note and ideas for cardholders help to make science "hands on" for everyone.

Science for Me will allow you to make science discovery rather than memorization of facts. Instead of giving solutions to problems, you can now provide opportunities to help children find their own routes to discovery.

HELPFUL HINTS

Science for Me is designed to be taken apart and used in the classroom. The science recipe cards are printed on heavy stock for durability and are ready to be cut in half and laminated or covered with clear Con-Tact paper. Cards can also be colored before you cover them. Each set of cards has been numbered for proper sequencing as well as picture coded for easy identification. Materials and tools should be placed in front of each card so that children can walk past each card "reading" and following the directions with little or no adult help. Start with the simple activities that have fewer steps and help children build independence and confidence as you move on to the more complicated activities. Experiments can be repeated to help all children achieve mastery and skill development.

It is best to work with a few children at a time. Make a copy of the waiting list sheet on page viii. Post this sheet at children's eye level to help everyone wait for his/her turn. Allow enough time for children to work at their own pace and to complete every step as the cards tell them.

Consider putting together science kits using the *Science for Me* cards. Cards, equipment, and supplies can be sorted in individual boxes and will be ready to set up on rainy days or for any other special time.

The letter to parents on page vii can be copied and sent home to encourage parents to become a part of the child's science exploration. You might even consider loaning a set of the cards to parents so that they can experience *Science for Me* at home.

Use *Science for Me* on a daily basis and help your students begin to understand the joy and excitement of the world of science.

CARDHOLDER IDEAS

CLOTHESPIN HOLDERS:

Mix a small amount of plaster of Paris and pour into small paper cups, candy cups, or similar containers. Using wooden spring-type clothespins, stick half of the top of a clothespin into the wet plaster. Leave the other end half extended out over the cup (bottom of the pin should be pointing up). Allow to dry. Attach a science card to the holder by opening the pin and attaching it to the center of the card.

DOWEL HOLDERS:

Use small wooden blocks and dowels. Attach dowels to the center of each block. Tape science cards to the dowel or attach Velcro-type tape to the dowel and the backs of the cards.

ACCORDION HOLDER:

Glue science cards to the center of tagboard or poster board squares (5" x 7"). Attach boards to each other with tape in an accordion-style format.

TENT STYLE:

Attach a stiff board back to each card using tape at the top of the card. Use the stiff board to support the card as it is set up on the table.

GA1318

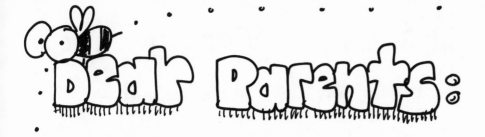

Dear Parents:

During the year your child will be participating in a special science curriculum called *Science for Me*. The activities in this curriculum allow children to experience science on a personal basis. Science activities are set up at individual stations where your child can follow picture cards to complete a science activity. This "hands-on" type of experience helps make the world of science much more meaningful and exciting for children.

You can help with these special activities by collecting some of the materials required for some of the experiences. We need baby food jars with lids, small aluminum pie plates, eyedroppers, newspaper, pieces of clay pot or pottery, small plastic drinking cups, plastic six-pack soda holders, and plastic berry baskets.

Please feel free to come in and look at some of the science recipes we will be using. I hope you will also talk with your child about the special science projects he/she will bring home.

GA1318

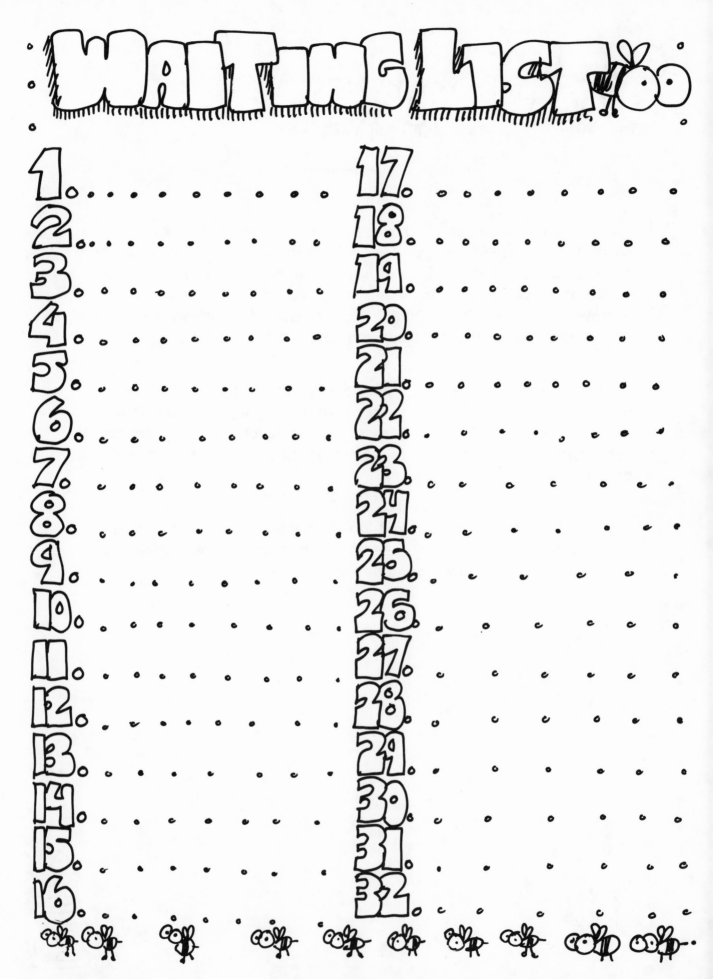

WAITING LIST

1. . . . .
2. . . . .
3. . . . .
4. . . . .
5. . . . .
6. . . . .
7. . . . .
8. . . . .
9. . . . .
10. . . . .
11. . . . .
12. . . . .
13. . . . .
14. . . . .
15. . . . .
16. . . . .

17. . . . .
18. . . . .
19. . . . .
20. . . . .
21. . . . .
22. . . . .
23. . . . .
24. . . . .
25. . . . .
26. . . . .
27. . . . .
28. . . . .
29. . . . .
30. . . . .
31. . . . .
32. . . . .

GA1318

CRYSTAL GARDENS

Objective: To help children understand how crystals are formed

Teacher's notes: **What Happens**: Crystals are formed as the solution moves into the porous material and the water evaporates (passes from liquid to a gas). The solid salt remains and forms crystals. When the liquid is gone, the crystals stop growing.

*Crystals will begin to form in about one hour and will reach their peak in about three or four days.

*The crystals are fragile, but allow children to touch one time to feel how soft and powdery they are.

*Caution children to use a very small amount of food coloring—too much color will only run together and turn to brown.

*Liquid bluing, which is needed in the solution, can be located in most grocery or drugstores. The following is one resource for liquid bluing:
Luther Ford & Co.
100 North 7th Street
Minneapolis, MN 55403

CRYSTAL GARDENS

Supplies needed:

1 baby food jar per child (Label with each child's name.)

measuring spoons
eyedroppers
food coloring
water
porous materials: pieces of lava rock, Styrofoam, sponge, cork, clay pot, or charcoal briquette

ammonia
non-iodized salt
liquid bluing

Crystal garden solution:

Makes 8-10 gardens.
1 cup non-iodized salt
1 cup water
Mix well. Some salt will not dissolve.

1 cup liquid bluing
4 tablespoons ammonia

1

GA1318

2

Choose materials and fill the jar ½ full.

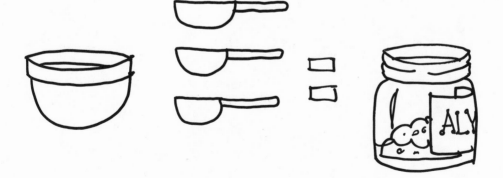

Add three (3) tablespoons of the crystal solution.

4

Add two (2) drops of food coloring.

Put your jar in a special place and watch your garden grow.

6

SALAD SEEDS

Objective: For children to become aware of seeds that can be eaten as sprouts

Teacher's notes: *An adult may punch the holes in the lids before the activity or allow older children to do their own lids with adult supervision.
*It is best to rinse the seeds several times each day. Your sprouts should be ready in about three days.
*Use your sprouts in a green salad or on top of cream cheese sandwiches.

Supplies needed:

1 baby food jar with lid per child
small hammer
thin nail
board to place lid on
alfalfa seeds (¼ teaspoon per child) soak seeds overnight before using
water in a bowl or large measuring cup
empty container to hold water that is poured from the seeds
  (Recycle this water back to the measuring cup or bowl.)
masking tape and waterproof pen to label jars
tray for the jars
salad or sandwich ingredients for eating sprouts

SALAD SEEDS

card 1

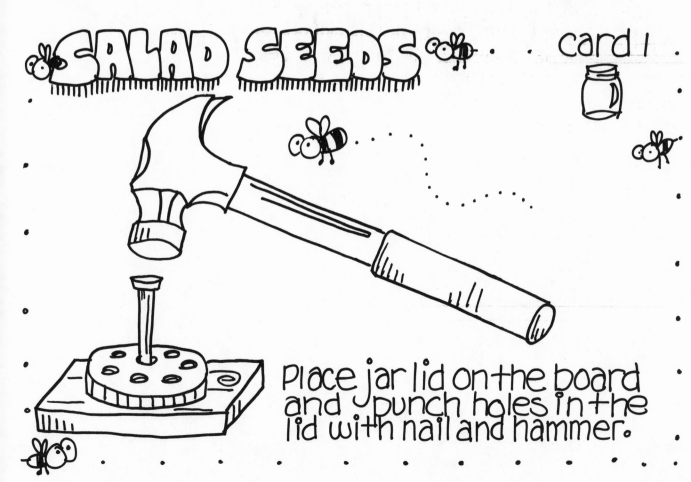

Place jar lid on the board and punch holes in the lid with nail and hammer.

GA1318

8

SALAD SEEDS · card 2

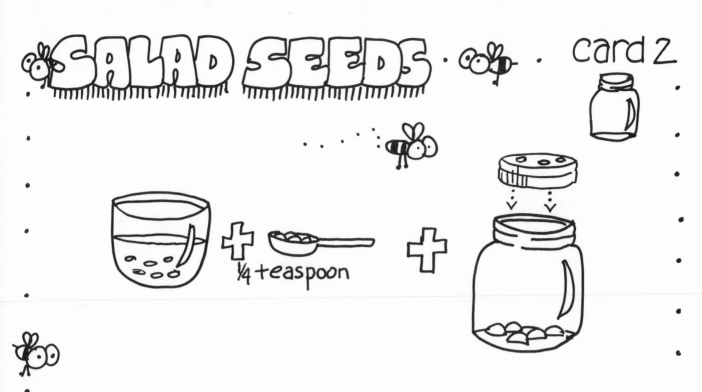

Add ¼ teaspoon of wet seeds to the jar.

SALAD SEEDS · card 3

(2) Two tablespoons of water

Add two (2) tablespoons of water. Cover the jar.

9

GA1318

10

GA1318

SALAD SEEDS card 4

Rinse the seeds and pour
the water into the bowl.

SALAD SEEDS card 5

Label the jar with the tape. Place your
jar on the tray.

GA1318

12

GA1318

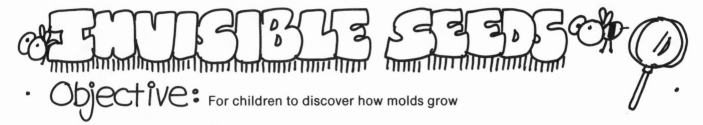

INVISIBLE SEEDS

- ## Objective: For children to discover how molds grow

- ## Teacher's notes:

What Happens: Invisible mold "seeds" called spores are everywhere around us. The right seeds, given the right conditions (dark, damp places and food), will cause the spores to grow. The spores use the soup for food. As they grow they produce more spores (seeds) which fall on parts of the soup and grow into new mold plants.

- *What are you looking at? Black mold—most common bread mold. Orange or reddish—neurospora mold. Bluish-green mold—penicillium mold
- *Some breads are made with preservatives in it to keep from getting moldy. Use bread crumbs from bread without preservatives.
- *Place the jars that have been "planted" with spores in a dark, warm area for about three days. Use magnifying glasses to observe the growth each day.

- ## Supplies needed:

1 baby food jar with lid per child
canned tomato soup
plastic wrap
small containers of bread crumbs and dirt

tape and pen to label jars
measuring spoons
tray to set jars on
magnifying glass
towel to clean hands

INVISIBLE SEEDS .card l

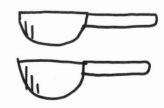

(2) Two tablespoons of tomato soup

Label jar with your name. Add two (2) tablespoons of tomato soup.

14

Plant your seeds. Sprinkle a little bread and dirt on top of the soup.

INVISIBLE SEEDS · card 3

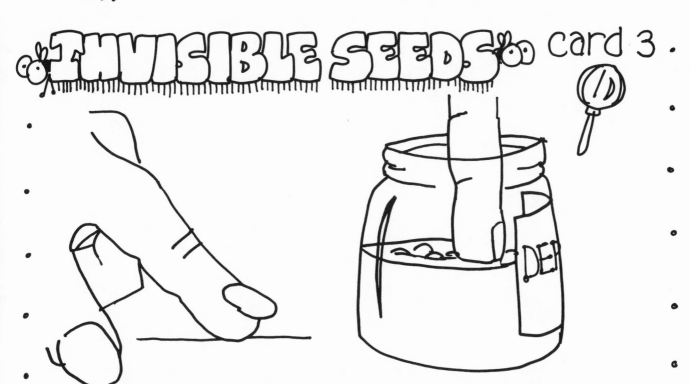

Rub your finger across the floor and touch the soup with your finger.

16

INVISIBLE SEEDS · card 4

Cover with plastic wrap and the jar lid.

INVISIBLE SEEDS · card 5

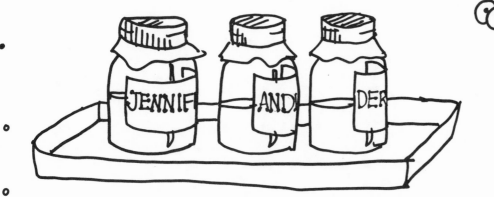

Place your garden on the tray and watch it grow!

17

GA1318

18

MARVELOUS MAGNETS

Objective:
To help children understand that objects made of iron or steel are drawn to magnets

Teacher's notes:
*Thousands of years ago, ancient man discovered that a gray-black rock would cling to the point of a spear. The rock was called lodestone and actually consisted of iron and oxygen, which made it a natural magnet. The name *magnet* refers to the Greek province of Magnesia where lodestone was found in abundance. Lodestone is also called magnetite and can be found in stores carrying science materials.

Supplies needed:
several large magnets
a variety of small objects—pennies, buttons, paper, foil, cork, wood, plastic, nuts, bolts, chalk, cloth, seeds or beans, paper clips, etc.
container to hold objects
attract and repel cards

MARVELOUS MAGNETS

Activity extensions:

You can help your students better understand the meaning of attract and repel by doing some creative movement activities.

1. Have students clasp their hands together when you say *attract*. Move their hands a part when you say *repel*. Increase the speed of your commands for some extra fun.
2. Pair your students and have them try to attract as many body parts as they can. Can they attract some parts and repel others?
3. Move outside, pair up, and form a circle. Pairs should lock arms back to back (attract position). When you shout *repel* everyone must find a new partner and get in the attract position before you shout *repel* again.
4. When outside, form a human horseshoe magnet and move as a group to an object. Have the group decide whether they should attract to repel the object.

20

GA1318

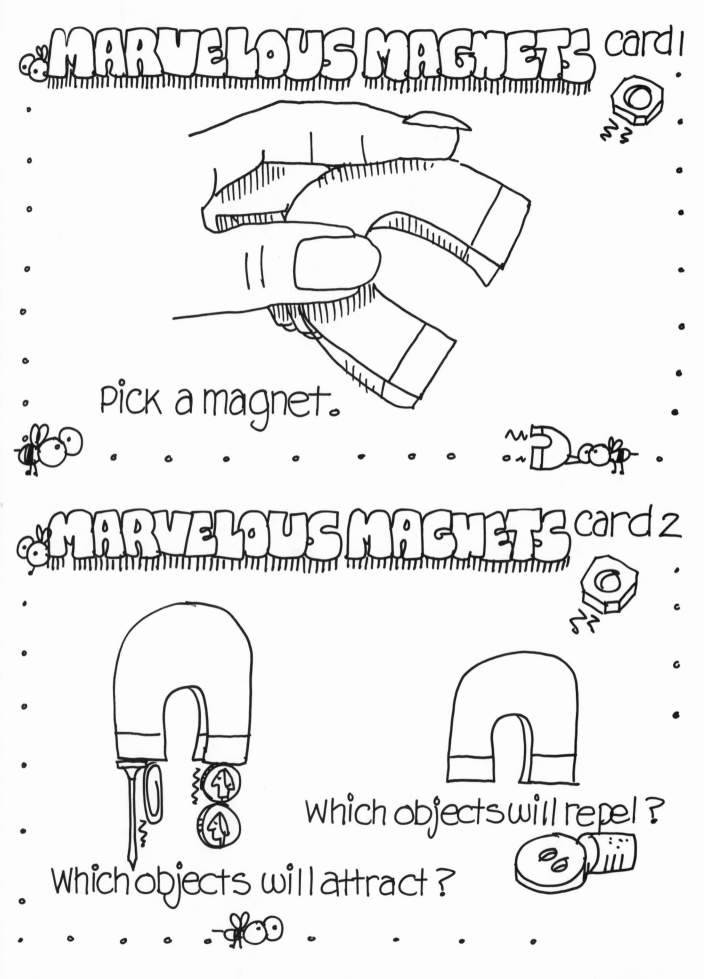

MARVELOUS MAGNETS card 1

Pick a magnet.

MARVELOUS MAGNETS card 2

Which objects will repel?

Which objects will attract?

21

GA1318

22

GA1318

MARVELOUS MAGNETS

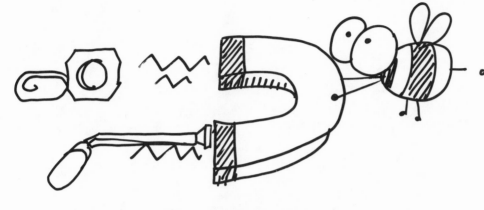

ATTRACT

MARVELOUS MAGNETS

REPEL

23

GA1318

GA1318

MAKE A MAGNET

Objective: To help children become aware that some metal materials can become temporary magnets

Teacher's notes:

What Happens: Many metals can be magnetized but they will only hold their magnetism for a short time. They contain some amount of iron and oxygen that helps to retain the properties of magnetism.

*Demonstrate the correct way to stroke the wire or nail before your students try this activity. You should stroke the nail or wire with a magnet in the same direction at least sixty times.

*You can make your own steel filings by cutting a steel wool pad into tiny pieces. Store your filings in a film can or prescription bottle.

You can make a piece of steel wire by pulling apart a paper clip.

Supplies needed:

2 large, strong magnets
steel nail or wire
several magnets of different sizes

steel filings
paper clips
box to hold steel filings

MAKE A MAGNET · card 1

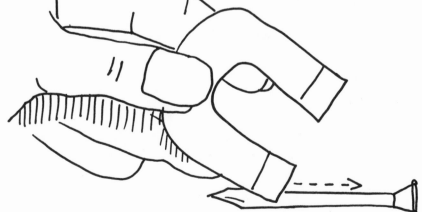

Rub magnet on nail or wire 60 times.

GA1318

26

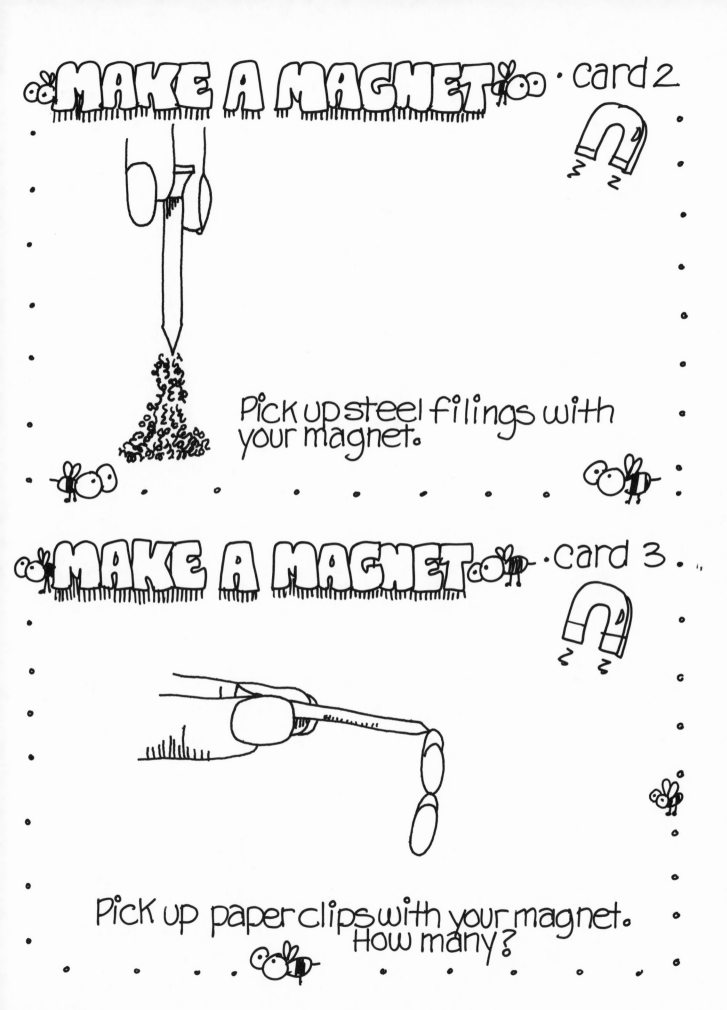

MAKE A MAGNET · card 2

Pick up steel filings with your magnet.

MAKE A MAGNET · card 3

Pick up paper clips with your magnet. How many?

27

GA1318

28

MAKE A MAGNET · card 4

Rub nail or wire again with magnet 60 times.

MAKE A MAGNET · card 5

Which magnet is strongest?

30

GA1318

MIGHTY MAGNETS

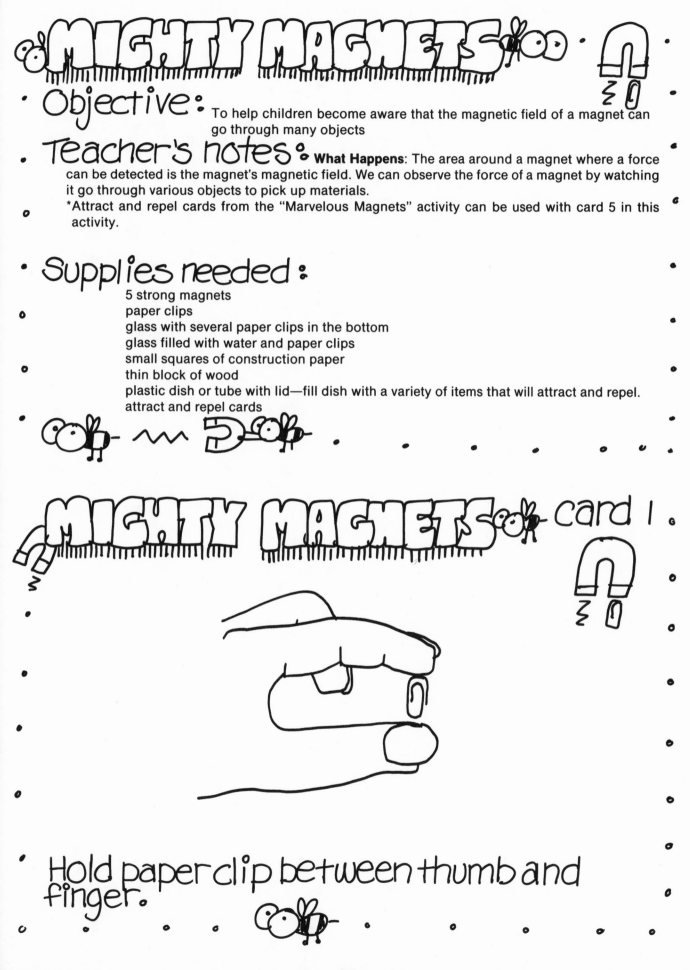

Objective: To help children become aware that the magnetic field of a magnet can go through many objects

Teacher's notes: **What Happens**: The area around a magnet where a force can be detected is the magnet's magnetic field. We can observe the force of a magnet by watching it go through various objects to pick up materials.

*Attract and repel cards from the "Marvelous Magnets" activity can be used with card 5 in this activity.

Supplies needed:

5 strong magnets
paper clips
glass with several paper clips in the bottom
glass filled with water and paper clips
small squares of construction paper
thin block of wood
plastic dish or tube with lid—fill dish with a variety of items that will attract and repel.
attract and repel cards

MIGHTY MAGNETS — card 1

Hold paper clip between thumb and finger.

31

GA1318

32

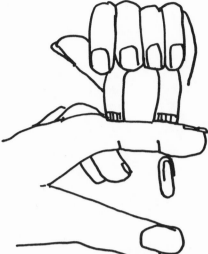

Hold magnet on top of finger and move thumb away. What happens?

Hold magnet next to glass. Can you move what's inside the glass?

34

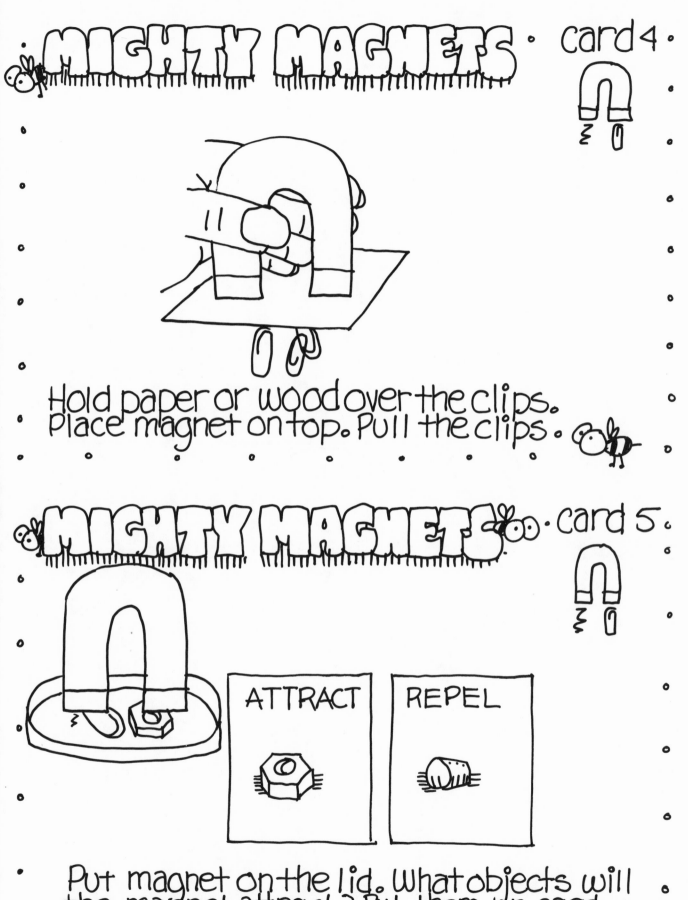

MIGHTY MAGNETS · card 4 ·

Hold paper or wood over the clips.
Place magnet on top. Pull the clips.

MIGHTY MAGNETS · card 5 ·

ATTRACT

REPEL

Put magnet on the lid. What objects will
the magnet attract? Put them on card.

35

36

BUBBLE MACHINE

Objective: To help children discover why bubbles pop

Teacher's notes:

What Happens: Dryness is a bubble's worst enemy. Touch it with something dry and it will break. We add glycerine to the bubble solution to try to help the bubbles last longer. Glycerine is a chemical used in hand lotions to help the skin from drying out. Glycerine added to a bubble solution keeps the bubble from evaporating too quickly.

*Add a little water to the cookie sheets or trays so the bubbles will not pop as they touch the tray.

*Have extra bubble solution on hand so that the bubble machines can be refilled. A recipe for the solution in larger quantities can be found on the Teacher's notes card for the "Bubble Tools" activity.

Supplies needed:

1 cup per child	2 plastic straws per child
1 square of aluminum foil per child	small pitcher of water
liquid dish soap	glycerine
measuring spoon	measuring cup
3 cookie sheets or trays	eyedropper
	bowl of water

BUBBLE MACHINE card 1

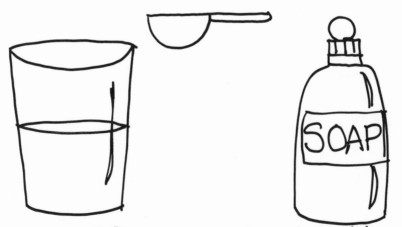

Take one (1) cup and add: ½ cup water, one (1) tablespoon soap

GA1318

38

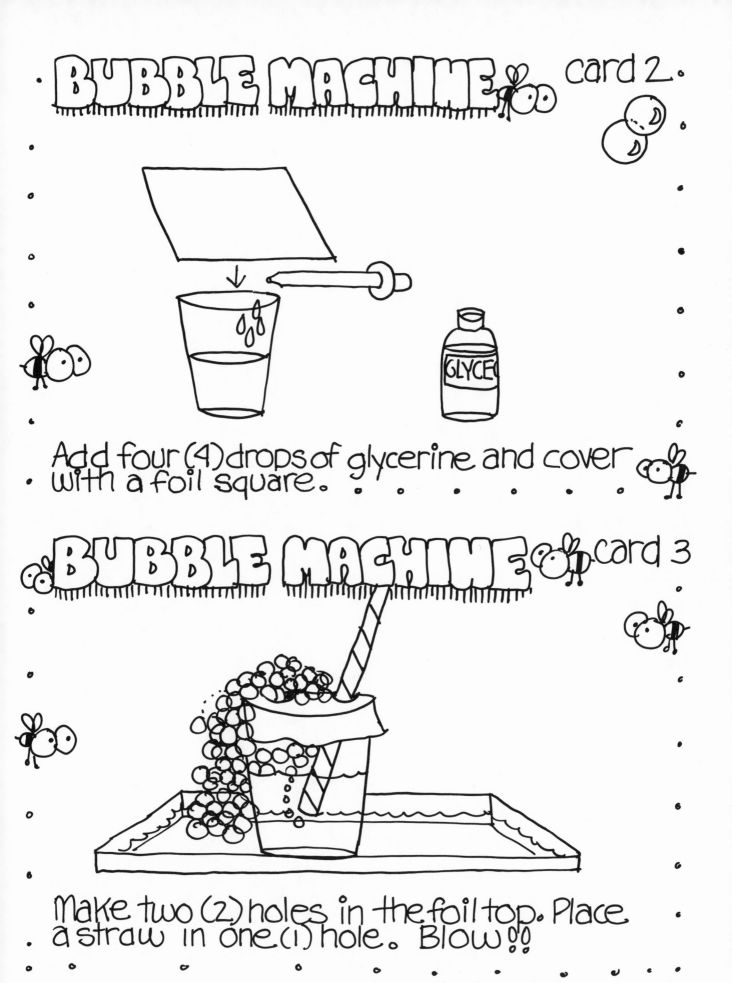

BUBBLE MACHINE · card 2·

Add four (4) drops of glycerine and cover with a foil square.

BUBBLE MACHINE card 3

Make two (2) holes in the foil top. Place a straw in one (1) hole. Blow!!

39

GA1318

40

BUBBLE MACHINE · card 4

Blow bubbles. Push straw through a bubble. What happens?

BUBBLE MACHINE · card 5

Blow another bubble. Wet straw tip. Push wet straw through bubble. What happens?

41

42

BUBBLE TOOLS

Objective:
To help children understand why soap bubbles last longer than plain water bubbles

Teacher's notes:

What Happens: Soap added to the water gives more space between water molecules. This space and the oil found in the soap help bubbles evaporate slower. Plain water bubbles evaporate too quickly and pop right away. Colors in bubbles are caused from light bouncing off the many different layers that are found in soap film. We see different colors because the layers are uneven. The thickest parts bounce back red, thinnest parts violet.

*An adult may need to help younger children tie the knot in the string for their bubble frame. Make sure the knot goes inside one of the straws.

*Caution children not to put their soapy hands in their eyes or mouth. Have plain water and towels on hand to help with any problems.

BUBBLE TOOLS

Supplies needed:

bubble solution (recipe below)
2 straws per child
towels
a tub of plain water (card 3)

1 pipe cleaner per child
1 25" piece of string per child
a variety of bubble tools
2 tubs of bubble water (cards 4 and 5)

Bubble tools solution:

(Dawn, Joy, and Ajax are the three liquid detergents that seem to make the strongest bubbles. They are also biodegradable.)
1 part liquid dish soap
1 part glycerine
4 parts water
Mix together and allow to sit overnight. This solution can be covered and stored in a cool place for several days.

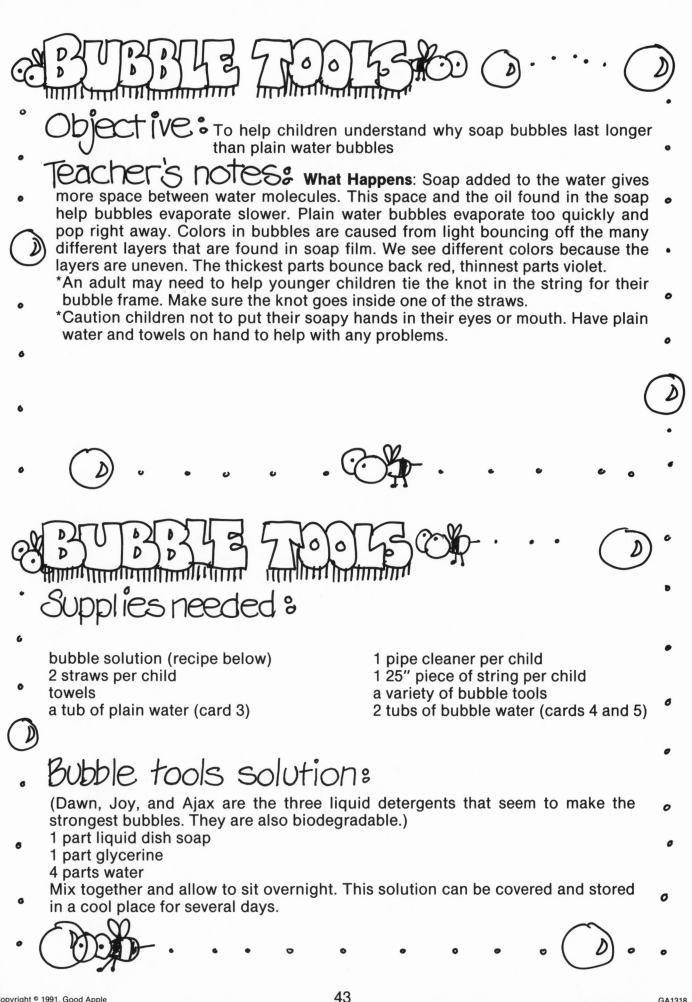

GA1318

44

GA1318

BUBBLE TOOLS

Simple items found around the house can make wonderful bubble blowers.

Juice can:
Remove both ends of can. Dip one end in the bubble solution and blow from the other end. You can tape several cans together to make bubble horns.

Paper cup:
Poke a hole into the bottom of a paper cup. Dip the open end of the cup into the bubble solution and blow gently through the hole.

Plastic funnel:
Dip the large end of the funnel into the solution and blow through the smaller end.

Six-pack holder:
A plastic six-pack holder can be dipped into the solution and gently waved through the air.

Plastic berry basket:
Cut the bottom from a plastic berry basket and hold it with a wooden clothespin. Dip in the solution and blow or wave through the air.

Remind children that the size of the bubble does not always depend on how hard they are blowing through their bubble tools. The way the mouth is shaped and how the air enters the bubble is very important. Help children experiment with their own bubble-blowing techinques.

BUBBLE TOOLS ... card 1

Take one(1) pipe cleaner. Bend it to make your own bubble wand.

45

GA1318

46

GA1318

BUBBLE TOOLS ... card 2

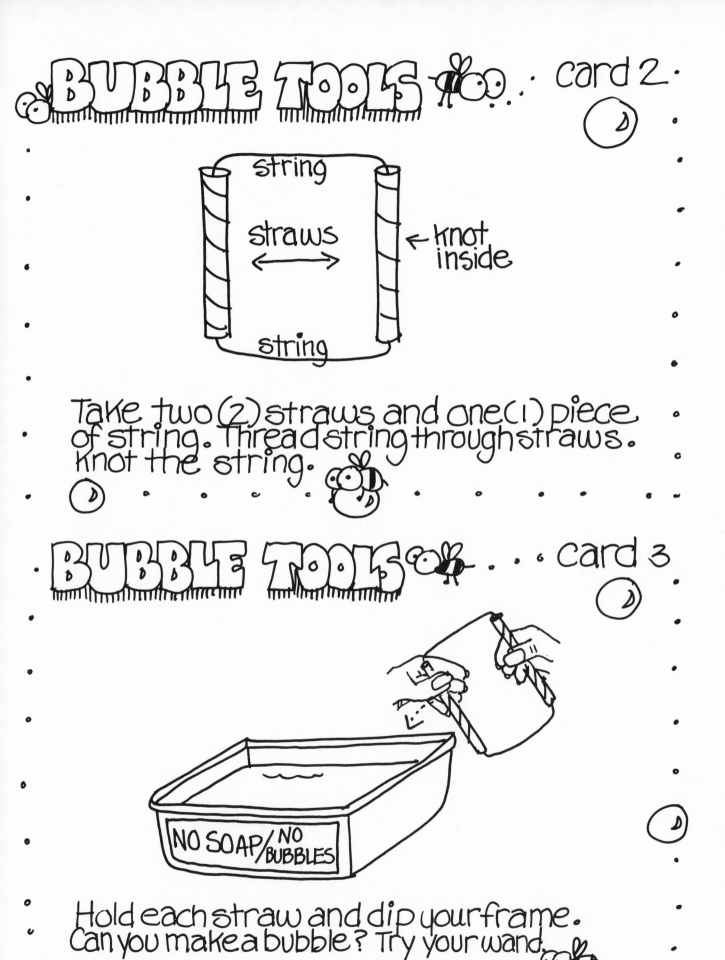

string

straws ←

knot inside

string

Take two (2) straws and one (1) piece of string. Thread string through straws. Knot the string.

BUBBLE TOOLS ... card 3

NO SOAP / NO BUBBLES

Hold each straw and dip your frame. Can you make a bubble? Try your wand.

GA1318

48

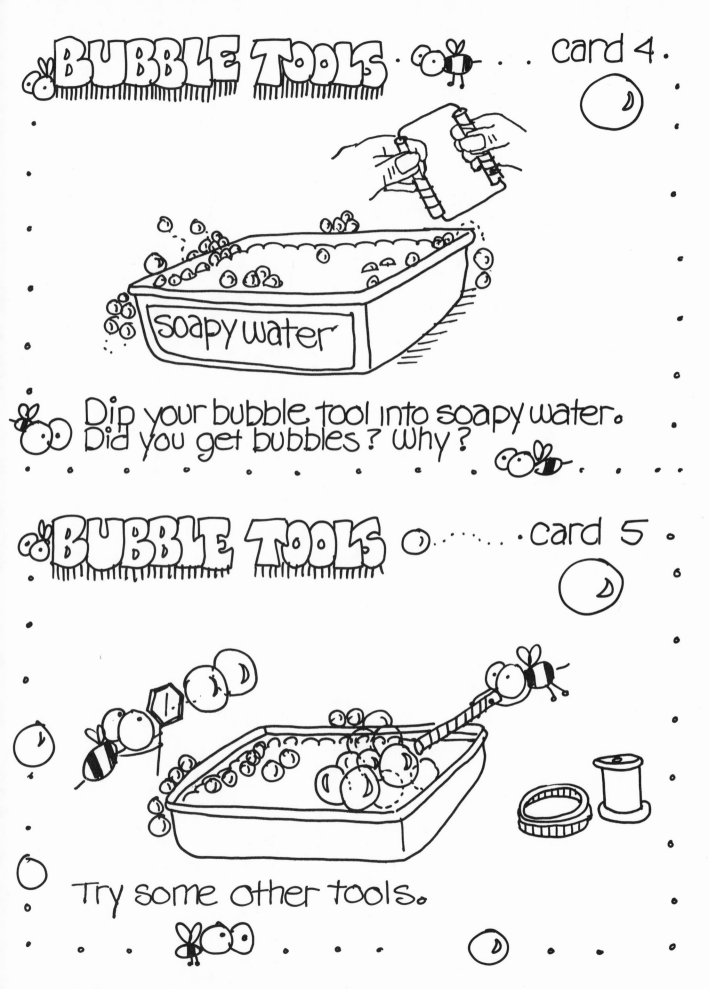

BUBBLE TOOLS · · · · card 4 ·

soapy water

Dip your bubble tool into soapy water.
Did you get bubbles? Why?

BUBBLE TOOLS · · · · card 5 ·

Try some other tools.

49

50

Objetive: To help children begin to understand the concept of surface tension

Teacher's notes:

What Happens: Water and other liquids have a thin film that covers their surface. Forces in the water surface (surface tension) pull the water molecules closer together and make the water seem to have a skin.

*The "skin" created by surface tension is able to stretch so that water poured into a cup will look as though it is stretching beyond the top of the cup.

*Surface tension on top of water will actually hold things up that normally sink in the water. When the surface tension is broken in some way, the object will sink.

*Use the Water Drop Chart to give children an opportunity to estimate how many drops they will need to add before the surface tension has reached its stretching capacity. You might want to cover your chart with plastic after you have written your students' names on the chart. Children can use a wipe-away pencil to write down their estimates. Convert your table chart to a large wall chart and have children use large raindrops to represent their estimations.

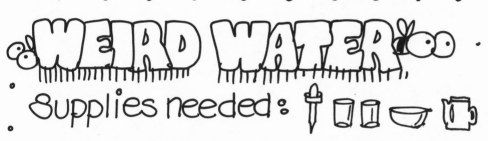

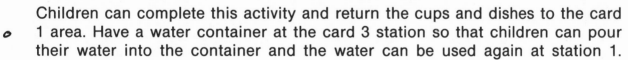

Supplies needed:

Children can complete this activity and return the cups and dishes to the card 1 area. Have a water container at the card 3 station so that children can pour their water into the container and the water can be used again at station 1.

several small cups or glasses
saucers, pans, or dishes to be placed under the cups to catch spills
small pitcher filled with water
container to hold water to be "recycled"
water drop chart to be placed between cards 3 and 4
eyedroppers
towels or newspapers for cleanup

GA1318

52

GA1318

WEIRD WATER . . . card 1.

Take one (1) cup and one (1) saucer.

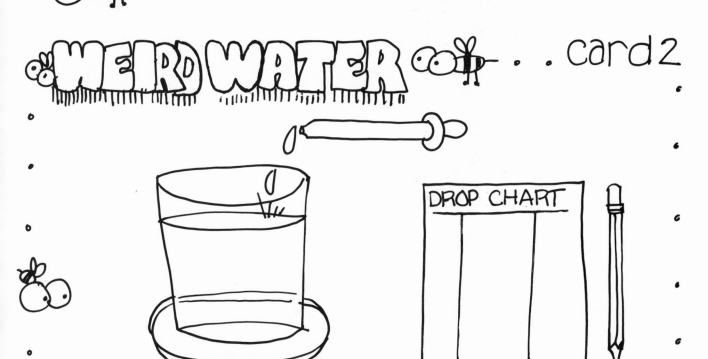

WEIRD WATER . . . card 2

Fill the glass to the top. Write down your drop estimate on the drop chart.

53

54

WEIRD WATER · card 3

Add water drops and watch your water "stretch." Count the drops.

WEIRD WATER · card 4

DROP CHART

BEAU	110	85
MELEA	95	
RORY	60	
JANA	112	

Write down how many drops you added. Pour water back.

GA1318

56

WEIRD WATER
Water Drop Chart

Name	Estimate	How many did it take?

GA1318

58

STICKY WATER

objective:
To help children develop an awareness that water will "stick" to itself and change shape

Teacher's notes:

What Happens: Water is continuously trying to pull itself together. When drops of water stick together or pull at each other, it is called *cohesion*. Drops of water are formed through cohesion.

*The wax paper allows the water drops to move freely to join together, but the water is not able to stick to the paper.

Supplies needed:

eyedroppers
wax paper squares

pitchers of water
paper towels to dry hands

STICKY WATER · card 1

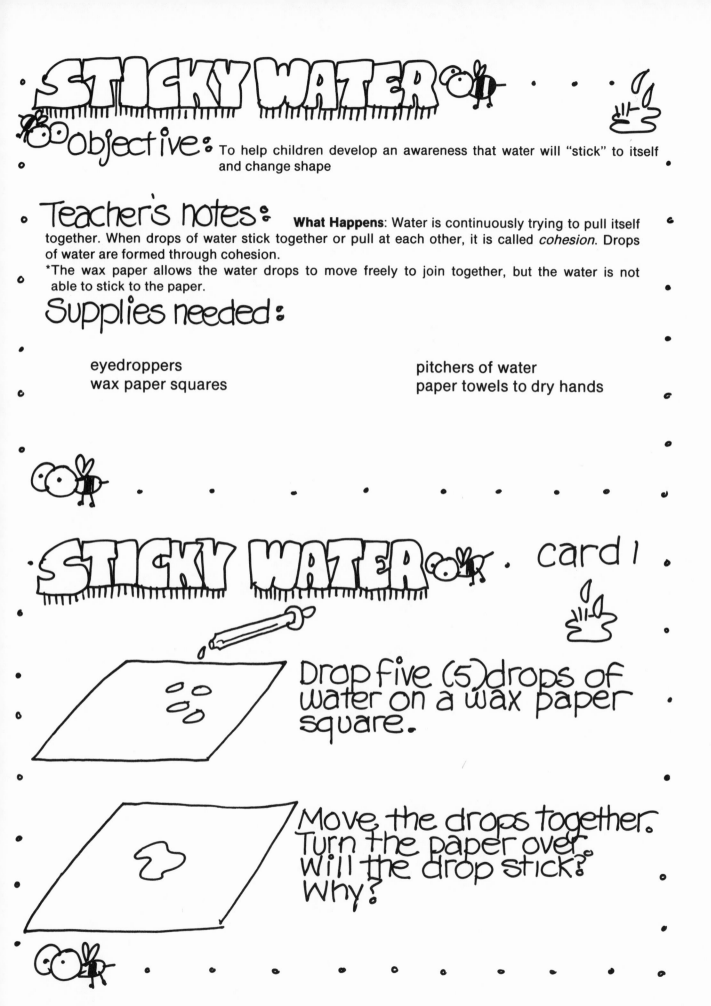

Drop five (5) drops of water on a wax paper square.

Move the drops together. Turn the paper over. Will the drop stick? Why?

59

GA1

STICKY WATER · card 2 ·

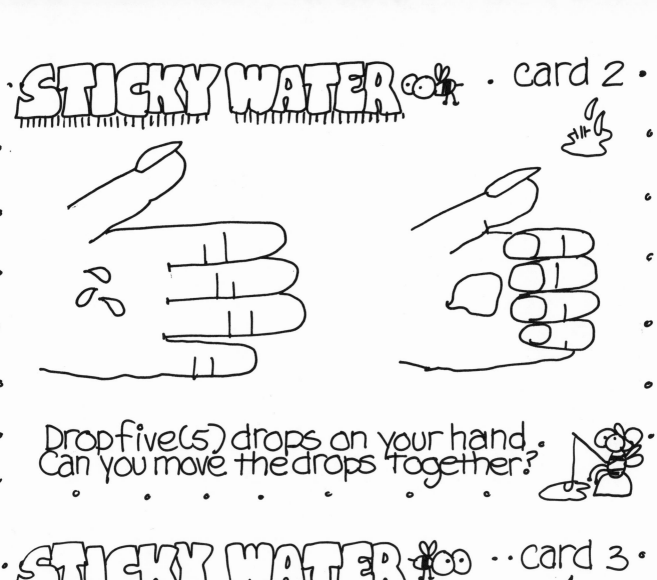

Drop five (5) drops on your hand. Can you move the drops together?

STICKY WATER ·· card 3 ·

Drop one (1) drop on your finger. Can you change the drops shape? Will the drop stick to your finger?

GA1318

62

FANCY FLOATERS

Objective: For children to develop an awareness of what can affect the surface tension of water

Teacher's notes: **What Happens**: Soap has oil in it. Oil breaks down the cohesive quality of water and this causes the pepper to scatter. Sugar will absorb the water and push the pepper back together again. The needle floats because the surface tension (the water's skin) has not been broken.

*Students may want to try these activities several times. It is good to have extra supplies on hand. Be sure that the needles and forks are dry before they are used.

*Many insects skim across a pond or lake because the surface tension of that body of water is strong enough to hold the weight of the insects.

*It is easier if you set up cards 4a and 4b together as one station.

FANCY FLOATERS

Supplies needed:

small bowls or pie pans
small towels to dry needles, forks, and hands
plastic forks
dish to hold wet needles
dish of liquid soap
dish of sugar
pan to hold water that has been used

pitcher of water
needles
pepper in a pepper shaker
eyedropper
measuring spoon (¼ teaspoon)

GA1318

64

FANCY FLOATERS

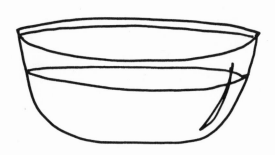

Fill the dish ½ full of water.

FANCY FLOATERS

Put the needle on the fork. Slowly lay the needle on the water. Water tension at work!

GA1318

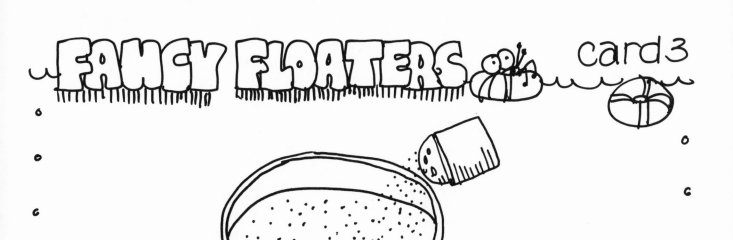

FANCY FLOATERS
card 3

Remove the needle. Sprinkle pepper on the water.

FANCY FLOATERS
card 4a.

SOAP

Add one (1) drop of soap. Watch!

GA1318

68

FANCY FLOATERS

Add ¼ teaspoon sugar. Watch!

FANCY FLOATERS

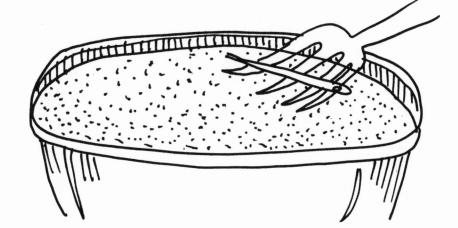

Lay needle on the fork. Will it float. again?

GA1318

70

GA1318

FREEZING FUN

Objective: For children to understand how salt lowers the freezing point of water

Teacher's notes:

What Happens: Salt will lower the freezing point of ice and cause it to melt. The water on the wet string is warmer than the ice. As the ice melts, it takes away enough heat from the water on the string to freeze the string to the ice cube. This is why salt is used to clear ice from sidewalks and roads. New drops of water on the string will dissolve the salt and release the string.

*You may have to demonstrate this activity to younger children before they try it on their own.

*Let your students practice picking up an ice cube just using the string without the salt. How many different ways can they think of to use the string?

Supplies needed:

several 9-oz. clear plastic drinking glasses
water in a child-sized pitcher
salt in a shaker
cotton string cut in 4" lengths (1 per child)
fresh water to dip string in
ice cubes
eyedroppers
container to pour used salt water and ice in

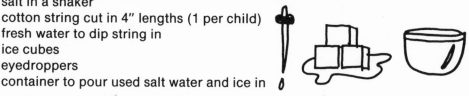

FREEZING FUN

card 1

Fill glass ½ full of water. Add one (1) ice cube.

GA1318

72

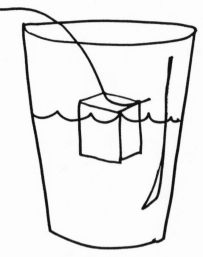

Take one (1) string and try to pick up ice cube.

FREEZING FUN · Card 3

Dip end of string in water & lay on top of the ice cube. Sprinkle with salt.

GA1318

74

FREEZING FUN

Count to thirty (30). Now lift your cube.

FREEZING FUN

Drop water on your string until it is loose again. How many drops did it take?

75

GA1318

76

CREEPING COLORS

Objective:
To help children understand that ink is made of different colored chemicals which move at different speeds

Teacher's notes:
What Happens: Inks and marking pens are often combinations of several colored dyes. The colors of inks and dyes are molecules of coloring substances that are dissolved in a liquid base. When the liquid creeps up the paper strip, it dissolves the coloring molecules and splits it into different colored chemicals. Different colors get carried along faster and farther than others because some color molecules are bigger and heavier than others.

*Older children might want to test ink using another type of liquid (alcohol) to see if the color patterns are different.

CREEPING COLORS

Supplies needed:

absorbent paper (coffee filters, paper towels, or newsprint)
water-soluble colored markers
scissors
1 clear plastic cup per child
water
tablespoon
1 paper towel per child
pencil/pen

The paper should be cut into strips 1" in width. You may want to mark the paper with 1" lines or precut the strips for younger children.
A 2" space should be left at the bottom of each strip when they are colored.
You may want to demonstrate how to color the strips.

GA1318

GA1318

CREEPING COLORS · card 1

Cut three (3) strips of paper.

CREEPING COLORS · card 2

ORANGE   PURPLE   GREEN

Choose three (3) markers and color
each strip near the bottom.

79

GA1318

80

CREEPING COLORS • card 3

Add two (2) tablespoons water to a cup.

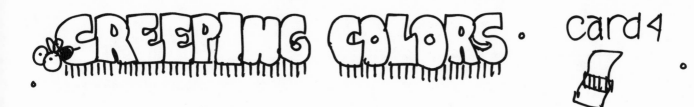

CREEPING COLORS • card 4

Set your colored strips in the glass.

82

CREEPING COLORS · cards 5 ·

Watch the colors move up the paper strips.

CREEPING COLORS · card 6

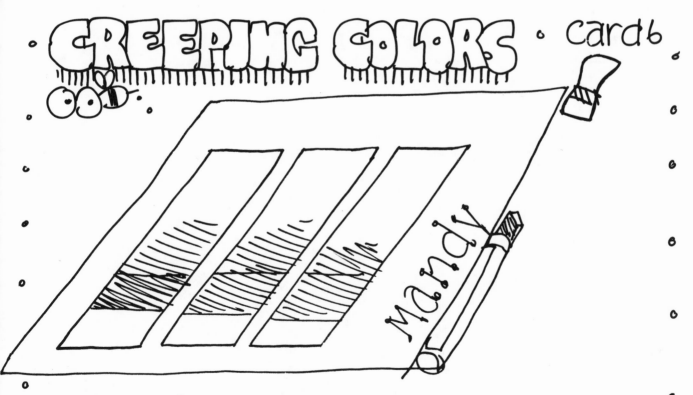

Lay strips on paper towel to dry. Write your name on the paper towel.

GA1318

84

GA1318

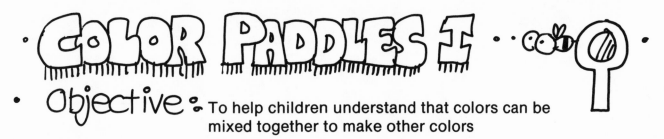

COLOR PADDLES I

Objective: To help children understand that colors can be mixed together to make other colors

Teacher's notes:

What Happens: The cellophane colors will blend together to make different colors. Red, blue, and yellow are primary colors and can be blended together to make other colors.

*Cut cellophane circles 1" larger than the pattern.

*Younger children may need help cutting the "window" out of the paddle. You can help by cutting a portion of the window away to get them started.

*Children will need to be careful not to get glue on the cellophane. You may want to demonstrate how to apply the glue. Try using sticks or cotton swabs.

*Card 3 comes with little color circles that will need to be colored in before they are laminated.

COLOR PADDLES I

Supplies needed:

- color paddle patterns
- pencils
- scissors
- thin cardboard, file folders work well (3 per child)
- precut cellophane circles, red, blue, green (1 per child)
- glue
- cotton swabs

COLOR PADDLES I — card 1

Trace three (3) paddles onto cardboard.
Trace a circle in the center of the paddle.

COLOR PADDLES I — card 2

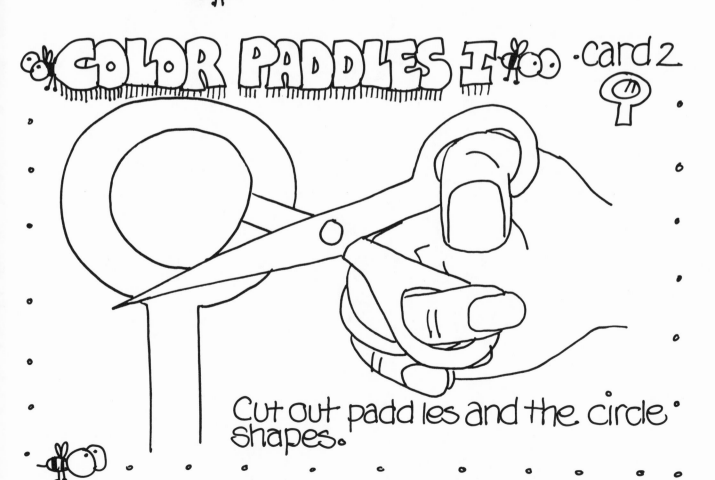

Cut out paddles and the circle shapes.

87

88

COLOR PADDLES I — card 3

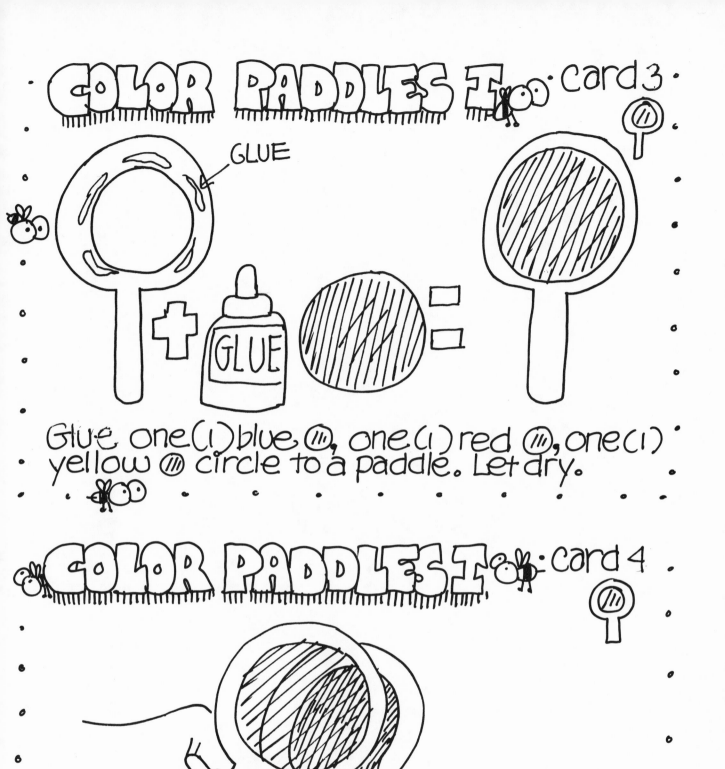

GLUE

Glue one (1) blue ⦿, one (1) red ⦿, one (1) yellow ⦿ circle to a paddle. Let dry.

COLOR PADDLES I — card 4

Hold your paddles together to make different colors.

PATTERN FOR COLOR PADDLE

91

92

 **COLOR PADDLES II**

Objective:
To help children develop an awareness that light is made up of colors

Teacher's notes:

What Happens: All of the colors we see are reflected colors. The colored cellophane in the color paddles acts as a filter stopping certain colors from reaching the eyes. It filters out all of the other colors from the light except the color of the filter. The red cellophane stops all colors except the red in white light. This makes the white paper look red and the red drawing seems to disappear. The green paddle allows only green light to reach the eyes. The red drawing will look black through the green cup because there is no green to reflect.

 **COLOR PADDLES II**

Supplies needed:

color paddles from the "Color Paddle I" activity
green and red pictures
red and green marking pens
drawing paper
The color paddles on cards 1 and 2 should be colored in with red and green to help nonreaders understand the activity.

93

GA1318

COLOR PADDLES II .. card 1 .

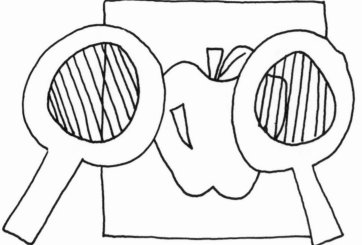

Use the red paddle to look at the red picture. Use the green paddle to look at the red picture. What happens?

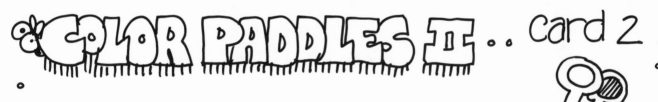

COLOR PADDLES II .. card 2

Use the green paddle to look at the green picture. Use the red paddle to look at the green picture. What happens?

96

GA1318

COLOR PADDLES II · card 3

Draw a design.

COLOR PADDLES II · · card 4 ·

Use your color paddles to look at your design. What happens?

GA1318

GREAT GOOP

Objective: For children to develop an awareness that some substances have the properties of both solids and liquids

Teacher's notes:

What Happens: *You might introduce the concepts of solid, liquid, and gas to the children before they make their Great Goop. Have samples of each kind of substance and review the similarities and differences of solids, liquids, and gases.

*A *property* can be defined as "the important characteristic of something."

*Anything that has weight and takes up room is matter. There are three kinds of matter:

    Solid—a piece of matter that keeps its shape

    Liquid—matter that has no shape of its own; it flows and pours.

    Gas—matter that has no shape at all; it can be collected in a closed container or it can spread out in the air.

*Have the children make a list of solids, liquids, and gases found in the room.

GREAT GOOP

Supplies needed:

1 baby food jar with lid per child
cornstarch
water
measuring cup
food coloring
spoons (not plastic)

bowl for the cornstarch
food coloring
measuring spoons
masking tape
pen

**Another good recipe is three parts glue to one part liquid starch.

GA1318

100

GA1318

GREAT GOOP

Label your jar with your name.

GREAT GOOP

+ two (2) tablespoons water

four (4) tablespoons cornstarch

CORNSTARCH

Add two (2) tablespoons water and four (4) tablespoons of cornstarch. Stir.

GA1318

102

GREAT GOOP

card 3

Add two (2) drops of food coloring. Stir.

GREAT GOOP

card 4

Touch and feel your goop.

103

104